HUNTING FOR CAIN

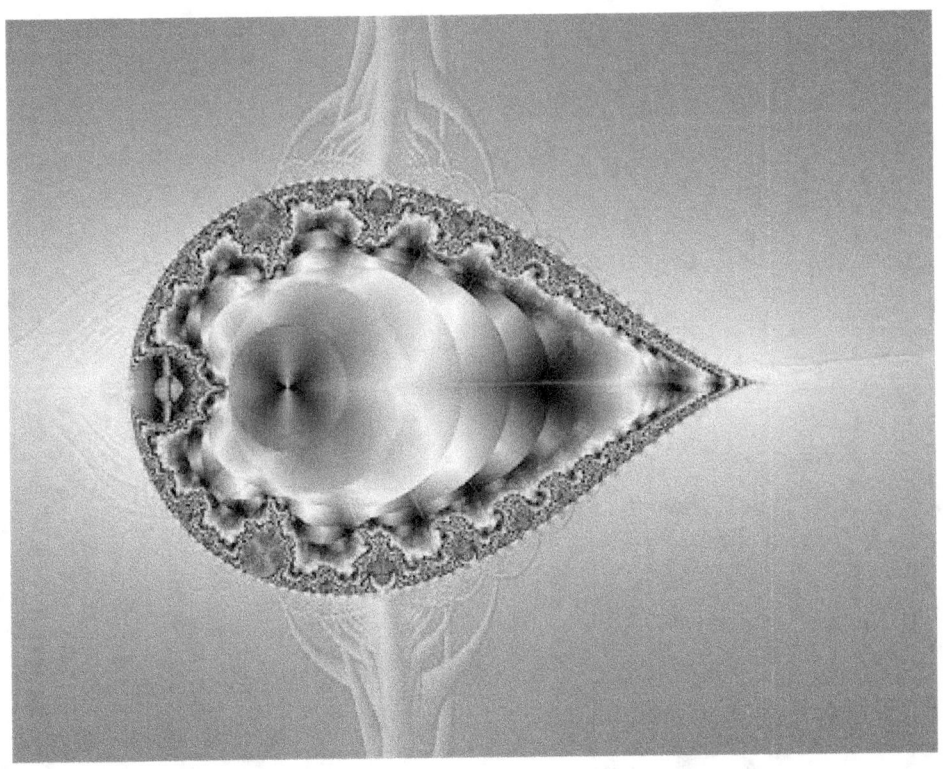

CONTENTS

Introduction

Western civilisation has multiplied the number of imaginary figures thanks to increasingly sophisticated technology capable of reproducing images, sounds and sensations in an instant. That which was a field of individual research up to a few decades ago is now shared by many and the contemporaneity of analyses, evaluations and emotions inevitably ends up affecting the critical ability of each and every individual.

The deep furrows made by science have determined the belief that imagination is a rival to reality in the conscience of us Westerners.

In this regard, science has represented religion's best ally. While the mind is constrained by the boundaries of sterile rationalism, the heart reacts with mystical emphasis and dogmatic projections. Dogma, faith, fanaticism and idealism are nothing more than natural reactions to an awkward, yet reassuring daily routine.

We take refuge in our hearts, so as not to lose the spice of life, but the mind and the heart probably had a different role in the original conception of the great builder.

Nowadays, our lives have become a desert, captive of perhaps the greatest manipulation managed by human ingenuity.

In the past, dictators subdued the masses using force or gifts. Yet this was not sufficient to stop the evolution of thinking and suppress the passion that drive the momentum of history towards different experiences and awareness.

Nowadays, thanks to the targeted use of technology, mankind's history has been halted and we are heading towards increasingly enormous internal and external catastrophes, unless some kind of intervention happens immediately to tear the facade of the subhuman level to which our minds and hearts have been driven.

As long as we continue to look for salvation outside ourselves, in a God, in an extra-terrestrial, in a guru or in a saviour of the masses, the probability of taking the path that we are destined for will become increasingly scant and we will be subjected to the inevitable manipulation of sophisticated minds.

The cosmic clock has already struck the hour of a new dawn, but mankind continues to persist in the shadow of its own conditioning.

There is a recent discovery of what could be gravitational spirals crossing the known universe. It is a concept that belonged to science fiction, but has now landed on the indoctrinated classrooms of science and is put forward as an evolution of empirical research. The discovery immediately did the rounds on the social networks and spread throughout the world. Many share it and some shyly comment on it, but few understand the profound sense and the extraordinary impact that the possible presence of gravitational waves, perceived as spirals, would have on our concept of time and space.

What if it were true that the entire solar system, which is in motion, like the known universe, is crossing, in a rotation of its own, an area of our fragment of the galaxy penetrated by unknown energy flows, sufficient to revolutionise known models and deeply affect our conscience? That discussion would mean entering the minefield of esoteric intuition, which is devoid of the credibility sought by our cognitive and rational Manichaeism.

The author of this book will avoid becoming embroiled in the debate that sees the classrooms of science, art and spirituality opposed to each other. Instead, the aim is quite another and that is to show that many of our projections are the conditioned reflex of something originating from our civilisation, from something that we no longer wish to see, from the vibrant movement that starts from below and aims high, albeit without certainties. It is therefore common sense to state that the one possible truth can solely be glimpsed if we start from within.

The hypothesis of alien civilisations

It was a summer's night, we were by the sea, in complete darkness, far from the bright lights of the city, brushed only by the breeze of the warm wind.

We contemplated the reflection of the starry sky on the brief lapping of the waves, a flash of orange shining on the water.

We suddenly shifted our gaze upwards, a triangular object bolted silently and quickly. Its movement was harmonious, like a large bird performing a dance in the sky.

We looked into each other's eyes, we remained in silence, as if inundated by energetic rain. We knew that we ad crossed paths with the unknown!

Reason tries to rationalise what happens, to lead it to the safety of a terrestrial explanation.

Science tells us that at the moment we are alone, that the possibility of another form of life in the universe is not excluded, that perhaps there are traces of water on Mars and that at the moment there is no proof of the existence of other planets which may have reproduced the conditions suitable for existence with any certainty. Billions of stars, unexplored galaxies, countless solar systems and planets: what would be their point? The answer to life beyond the Earth can only be affirmative, even just using simple statistical calculations that are part of science itself!

They make us believe that we confuse unidentified flying objects with satellites or aerostatic balloons, that technologically advanced radars do not perceive any noteworthy sound from the cosmos and that the X files are a cinematographic invention or, at best, a series of events which still lack full explanations.

The White House was inundated with requests for information on the phenomenon, on what happened in Area 51, on Roswell, on alleged contacts of former heads of state with alien entities, even confirmed by close relatives of the persons in question, but never, ever, has there been an official denial, a press conference to negate the circumstances.

It is evident that behind this approach is an awareness of the herd, of information policies aimed at misguiding the masses, of hidden, military and financial strategies, to bend the planet to the will of a select few.

It is not a matter of uncritical adhesion to conspiracy theories, it is simply a fact, made possible by technology and the manipulation of the media, even that which we assume to be independent, such as social networks.

However, it would be overly simplistic to observe the phenomenon and consider that manipulation on a worldwide scale and the hierarchical decisions regarding events that touch the lives of billions of people, artificially created wars, nations that fail and epidemics that then require the use of miraculous vaccines are the product of superior intelligence endowed with economic, political or Masonic power.

The reality is less obscure, simpler and not without a dose of undeniable drama.

It is all possible solely because the majority of mankind lives in a primitive, apparently limited consciousness, involved in a sort of behavioural hypnosis dictated by a fragmented state of the ego.

Therefore, returning to the subject of extra-terrestrials, ufology's presumption of explaining the evolutionary level of these beings and classifying them into actual races is totally flawed by obscurantism.

Accounts by persons who claim to have been contacted may also be the result of extrasensory experiences, which may have some foundation, but are precisely the reason they lack sufficient credibility. Credibility is not part of the scientific culture of proof, it is something quite different.

We do not know what happens up in the skies and we cannot easily reject the assumption that most of those intuitions are generated from down here, as projections of our fears and our aspirations.

I am convinced that, before long, the veil crossing the mysterious confines of reality that are unknown to us will be lifted by the flow of cosmic events and, sooner or later, this will prepare mankind for encounters with other, more advanced civilisations. However, if fragments of these civilisations are already in our midst, which might be probable, it is equally certain that the information in support of or against the various theories are totaly unreliable. Indeed, they are probably used for a number of obscure ends.

If someone is watching us, it is very plausible that they are doing so with a great sense of compassion, respecting our evolution and providing exclusively indirect assistance.

At the moment, we can note that we are even able to tame the unknown, according to varying degrees of perverse logic, each born of frustration and fear. If an alien god really existed and manifested itself to mankind, there would soon be a new religion and the enlightened message would be imprisoned in new temples, mosques or churches.

The three chakras

The New Age culture, which is typical of the Seventies, introduced different notions regarding the appearance and the meaning of the chakras to the West.

Indeed, in traditional Indian and Eastern literature, different systems are used to describe the chakras. This has resulted in the impossibility of venturing into the intricate study of the vital centres of the body without incurring the risk of confusion or unavoidable simplifications.

The chakra is an icon aimed at reinforcing the concept of the existence of vital nodes that interact with the slight bodies, acting as secret intermediaries between the visible and the invisible.

However, if we release ourselves from the seven chakras belonging to the ancient orientalist traditions, which are used positively by the practitioners of alternative medical sciences, such as acupuncture, and compare our ego with the three basic centres, the mind, the heart and the pelvis, we will also be better able to identify the various observation points of reality and intercept the portal through which to interpret the phenomena.

What could appear an attempt at summarising may, instead, end up representing an effective and coherent tool for understanding.

We shall attribute the common, well-known meanings to three vital centres, in which the mind is where events are processed, the heart is home to feelings and passions and the pelvis is the intersection of desires and instincts.

Cerebral, sentimental or passionate and instinctive are known human categories inscribed in books on psychology, but their meanings have forcibly entered the collective imagination as a result of logical evidence.

To understand the meaning of vital nodes, you need to have an overview of life as a known plane of existence. Obviously, the intended here is not to explore the paths already beaten by esoteric science, as I believe that a number of enlightened interpreters have already provided learned information on the subject.

The attempt is to use a few concepts to group the result of ancient investigations and knowledge that has withstood the test of time.

Hermes Trismegistus is one of mankind's great teachers. The Emerald Tablet represents the essence of his teachings. Entering into detail on the intuitions of Hermes is a revelation on how knowledge preceded

16

science and the latter constitutes a pale reflection of the former:

That which is below is like that which is above, and that which is above is like that which is below, to accomplish the miracle of One Thing. And all things have proceeded from One, by meditation of One, so all things are born from this One Thing, by adaptation. The Sun is the Father thereof, the Moon the Mother, the Wind carried it in its belly, the Earth is its Nurse. The Father of all the Telesme of the whole world is here. Its strength and power is complete if it be converted into earth. Separate the earth from the fire, the slight from the gross, gently and with unremitting care. It ascends from the earth to the heavens, and again descends to the earth and thereby gathers to itself the strength of things above, and of things below. By this means, all the glory of the world shall be yours and all obscurity shall flee from you. It is the strong strength of all strength, for it shall overcome every slight thing and penetrate every solid thing. Thus was the world created. Hence shall wonderful adaptations be achieved, of which the means is here. Therefore, I am called Hermes Trismegistus, for I hold three parts of the philosophy of the whole world.

Therefore, everything that is divided has a single source. Everything that appears to us can be multiplied on infinite scales, adapting it to the various planes of existence.

There is nothing inside us or outside us that is not reproduced on reality's different levels of representation.

This intuition allows us to travel among the secrets of the universe with lightness and amazement, without having to resort to the results of mundane experiments on the speed of light!

Therefore, adapting the principle to the three basic centres of our ego, it is not difficult to project this trichotomy onto a multitude of levels.

For example, our planet is also necessarily endowed with three basic vital centres that are invisible to the human eye. The North, identified as the Arctic and the countries below it, represents the head, the South, the Antarctic and the countries above it, represents the pelvis, and the countries in the middle, which represent the heart.

It is an undeniable fact that the Nordic countries are characterised by planning, order, production, logical analysis of events and that, prevalently, the inhabitants of these places have characteristics of detachment and self-control that pertain to the centres of the mind. Latin populations, on the contrary, are mainly driven by the passions of the heart, whereas tribal populations follow the instincts of the pelvis.

Even the subdivision of the planet into West and East is no more than the identification of the two lobes of the brain that respectively control the mind and the heart.

In my story entitled *La vita deserta*, the protagonist, called Giorgio, comes across a hand-written notebook during a trip to Vietnam.

The author, named Walter, describes an initiatory path through the various places on the planet.

Below is a faithful reproduction of a fragment of the narration that evocatively describes the concept:

Dear Monica, I hope to deliver this letter in person, maybe tomorrow or as soon as possible. Tonight I read more than half of the notebook that thanks to you I managed to have in my cell. I finished the part about Walter's journey. The history of his travels is the outward representation of an interior journey. The idea that our planet could coincide with the geometry of our bodies, identified not only in an anatomical sense, but also as an alchemical laboratory, in which the fragmentary and dualistic essence of existence finds its derivation in the separation between the mind and the heart had never crossed my mind. I discovered that during his travels in the West, Walter observed the left side of the brain, that of logical representations, of reasoning, of planning and efficiency. In the West, the brain glorifies the theoretical and intellectual virtues, apparently resolving conflicts in the planning of events through an analysis that comes from experience. Here, Walter observed the phenomenon of the mind that lies and unmasks the illusion of materialistic laicism. In the East, on the other hand, he encounters the right side of the brain that solves fear through images of the gods and paradises in the afterlife. Here is the home of fantasy, inspiration, legends, poets of pain and its populations find a solution to suffering in the transilluminated myths of reincarnation and mystic occultism. The South, on the other hand, is the bum of the world and the desolate Antarctic represents the solitude of an empty existence without boundaries. In the South, the populations experience primitive instincts and empty sentimentality to divert thoughts recycled from the past towards earthly passions. Here, the mind has never questioned itself, a victim of ferocious and violent adoration. Then, Walter reaches the North, which he had already crossed at the beginning of his journey, and rediscovers diversity, observes essence and recognises unity. Here, Walter meets Walter, the victory of the other, the end of every human desire, the revelation of the mystery...

Therefore, the three chakras represent the synthesis of a cosmic dimension that also involves our planet and its inhabitants.

The separation of the elements, due to the mystery of the fall, determined its fragmentation.

Common experience teaches us that the more balanced the vital components of a living organism, the greater balance there is. An excessive imbalance of certain factors to the detriment of others produces diseases, disharmony and psychic imbalances.

From the observation of the phenomena, without fear of approximation we can affirm that, generally speaking, two aspects of the three vital nodes are prevalent in any personality, obviously in terms of a proportional decrease which does not totally exclude the third.

In a personality that mainly concentrates on the satisfaction of instincts, with strong sexual urges, a lover of food and enjoyment, but at the same time inclined to sentimentality and passions, the chakras of the pelvis and the heart undoubtedly prevail, to the detriment of the chakra of the mind. Subjects committed to intellectual professions will primarily act with the chakra of the mind, whose potential is enhanced by the chakra of the heart or the pelvis, according to their inclination.

This will subsequently result in a search for compensation in human relationships. It is not uncommon to see particularly sensitive, sentimental people who are equally affected by a strong dose of

21

instinctiveness team up with personalities with a strong cerebral emphasis. An essay could be written on the relationships in couples related to their compatibility.

Further proof of how a phenomenon can adapt to various levels of representation of reality is provided by the evolution of mankind and its history. It would not be difficult to see the prevalence of certain aspects with respect to others in the various phases of human evolution, demonstrating the fact that the collective ego, identified in the various phases of history, is also subject to the same laws of this nature.

Therefore, the three chakras are separate. That is the snapshot of reality. Conflict between the various elements produces imbalance. Conflict is the cause of internal and external wars. That is why the ancient theosophists stated: *«It will never be possible to defeat war, unless we first resolve the wars we bear under our hats!»*.

Only a traveller of the soul can unify the three elements, restoring their original dignity. That's why one in whom is a trine!

All of these considerations are an essential introduction to the topic that we will discuss regarding the terrestrial civilisation and the races it consists of.

The slight dimensions

Western civilisation has relegated the invisible world to the cenacles of occultism and religious dogma. While the latter is accepted as an integral part of the system (many scientists also profess their religious faith), all that transcends the known world has deserted the classrooms of official knowledge and been marginalised to the realms of mystery, popular credulity and even folkloric magicism.

Negating the existence of invisible worlds is just as daft as seeking proof that we are not alone in the universe!

Perhaps a little clarity is needed on this aspect. Things we don't see are just as real as those we do and, paradoxically, that is exactly what science tells us!

If we watch a programme on TV, we do not expect to look out onto the balcony to view the images that the antenna captures out of the air! If we put a finger in an electrical outlet, we know precisely what the consequences could be, although the energy conveyed by the wires is invisible.

Electromagnetic radiation, X-rays, radio waves, the ionosphere and cosmic rays are just little examples of that which is invisible and there are thousands of other examples.

Cosmologists define dark matter as a component that cannot be seen, since, unlike known material, it does not emit electromagnetic radiation and appears through gravitational waves.

Science hypothesises that dark matter constitutes the majority, almost 90%, of mass present in the universe! Therefore, the obvious ignorance concerning the fields of the invisible can consequently be understood.

After all, imagining such a waste of space really would be a paradox! The obvious logical deductions of an elementary analysis such as this one are within everyone's grasp.

We do not have the sensory tools to perceive the invisible and this apparently condemns us to relying on the imagination or on information originating from teachers of occultism of varying ability. However, that really isn't the case!

As we shall see, logical reasoning provides us with the certainties that scientific evidence lacks.

Indeed, science itself resorts to paradox.

In this sense, atomic physics provides a glaring example. Atoms are not visible, but we derive their mass and charge from other experimental evidence! What is this evidence? It is not clear and if you read any book on quantum physics you will discover that, since it is not visible, data regarding an atom is a purely probabilistic concept!

Therefore, scientific reasoning relies on probabilities in order to negate the outcome of logical reasoning.

As early as the Fifties, astrophysicist Nikolai A. Kozyrev tried to demonstrate beyond doubt that such a source of energy must exist and that physical matter is made of an aether of invisible and conscious energy, but the Russian scientific community obviously did not take long to isolate him.

What is the aether?

The term "Aether" in Latin means "splendour" and the reality of the invisible energy that pervades the known universe has always been the foundation of teachings of mystery schools throughout the world.

The anagram of eter is net = fabric!

It is the "Ki" of the East.

Ancient philosophers such as Plato and Pythagoras already knew of its existence. Indeed, in ancient traditions the invisible world interacted with reality in spontaneous complicity and scientific modernism attributed the observation of these phenomena to mere superstition too hastily.

However, recent discoveries concerning the "dark mass" have obliged recalcitrant science to recognise that there must be a medium of energy hidden somewhere in the Universe.

Hence, talk of a "quantum medium" began. Obviously, the term "aether" could not be used because it was forbidden.

These gentlemen, belonging to a pre-established axis of power in scientific academies and who almost always receive massive funding from industries and politics, represent the true fortune tellers of this millennium!

After all, if official science were to recognise the existence of the ether, understood as matter existing in a different vibrational frequency and therefore constitutive of autonomous worlds, as being highly probable, all popular beliefs, religions, occultism and magic would be disproved in one fell swoop! Indeed, admitting that life also exists in the invisible realms, just as it does in the universe formed by dense matter, would mean providing concrete evidence regarding a series of phenomena on which religions built their fortunes.

Indeed, if every material body is surrounded by the aether, it follows that the traditional interpretation of the concept of death is totally fallacious and that, inevitably, according to the law of 'on earth as it is in heaven', once consumed, our bodies will continue to survive for a certain time in the aetheric sphere of the planet, according to a law that is totally natural and free of spiritual inflections.

Hence, we would understand phenomena such as apparitions, ghosts, mediumistic sessions and anything else to do with invisible spheres to which we unjustly attribute a magical significance. We would understand that just as we are ignorant "here", we continue to be so "beyond", and that every living entity follows an autonomous and independent evolutionary pattern.

The worlds of visible and invisible matter follow the same laws as those of this universe, they are the result of the same matrix and they pursue the same creative end that we can see in every aspect of nature.

They are both expressions of the limits of this nature, subject to transformation, change and death. Our Universe is a finite space that, in its continuous movement, is in search of infinity, the same infinity that poets and writers have been talking about for centuries, which escapes our understanding and the existence of which lies beyond the confines of our knowledge, in the unity that remains the ultimate desire of every authentic seeker.

The terrestrial races

Nowadays, classifying the various groups of human beings into races is considered politically incorrect as well as scientifically incorrect. Mankind's great disaster caused by Nazism, apartheid in South Africa and racial segregation in the United States of America has virtually nullified all references to race.

On the contrary, we will show no reticence when it comes to the concept of race and its proper meaning, namely the ability to identify groups of individuals linked by a single common denominator within the same species. In traditional taxonomy, the subdivision of human species was classified according to common genetic and hereditary traits, therefore primarily in reference to physical characteristics.

Skin colour, somatic features and body structure have always been the anthropological reference points in the study of the different types of human.

In truth, there is a finer substratum that differentiates human groups and is irrespective of the hereditary and genetic axis.

The reference is not to astrology. Astrology merely measures the potential of individuals as a result of their own past. The natal chart is the projection of our subconscious, which in turn is rooted in genetic structure, which in turn originates in the past. Therefore, the past is the cause.

My intention is to talk about the effect, about that which appears and limit the discussion to that which appears.

Semir Osmanagich is an American anthropologist, founder of the Bosnian park, the most active site in the world for archaeology enthusiasts.

He stated that:

Acknowledging that we are witness to fundamental proof of advanced civilizations dating back over 29,000 years and an examination of their societal structures forces the World to reconsider its understanding of the development of civilization and history. [...] Conclusive data at the Bosnian Pyramid site revealed in 2008 and confirmed this year by several independent labs who conducted radio carbon testing dates the site at 29,400 +/-400 years minimum.

Obviously, this discovery is only the tip of the iceberg of several studies on the subject that univocally contribute to determining the realisation that Plato was not a visionary and that Atlantis is not a fantasy that inhabits in the mind of some abstract creator of myths!

The realisation that the history of mankind on this planet is a great lie that has been written and recounted brings us back to the original question asked in the premise: is there an external figure who governs our lives and has an interest in keeping us ignorant? Instead, could it be that a human race with specific characteristics prevailed over others, determining group characteristics that tend towards self-mystification?

The tendency to look for an external God, to follow a religious, scientific or political authority, the aspiration to solve our insecurities through the construction of complex judicial systems, the tendency to imprison ourselves in sentimental relationships in the name of a ill-treated sense of love, the formation of philosophical thinking devoted to a systematic method and mankind's great park of distractions all appear as manifestations of a collective psyche that yearns for reassuring systems of life, but not for the truth.

A man who wishes to understand what freedom is must completely reject authority, and that is extraordinarily difficult, it takes great care. We can reject the authority of a guru, of a priest, of an idea, but we establish an authority within us, namely: "I think it's right, I know what I'm saying, it's my experience". Can the mind free itself from the authority and tradition that leads us to accepting another as a guide, or someone who tells you what to do? We obey and accept authority because within us there is insecurity, confusion, loneliness, and the desire to find something permanent, lasting. However, is there anything created by thinking that it is permanent and lasting?

It is this tendency in mankind, so admirably described by the great thinker Jiddu Krishnamurti, which encourages multidimensional occult powers in projects designed to ensnare mankind in preconceptions, prejudices and primitive obscurantism.

Paradoxically, human civilisation is the cause of its own prisons. Therefore, jailers exist because they know they can count on persons who are willing to be imprisoned. The great mystification and ignorance in which mankind survives have internal, not external origins.

Which is this race that now dominates?

In order to understand, and perhaps discover that it is not merely a literary theory, we must first make a hermeneutic effort on the various types of human.

I decided to use the imagery of ufology to show that the identification of the main extra-terrestrial races is merely the exterior, cosmic projection of terrestrial races present in the development of the various planetary eras.

In traditional ufology, the Reptilians, Greys, Nordics, Arturians are the main races of reference, therefore in the interests of brevity, those are the ones we will make reference to.

Studying the characteristics of these races will lead us to incredible discoveries and we will view the present with a different perception of the phenomena.

However, before commencing an analysis of the different types and understanding that these different races have been in our midst for millennia, indeed... they are us... we need to take a small step back and do justice to the ancient civilisation of Atlantis that, even now, we still struggle to deal with courageously and in the spirit of truth.

The garden of the Gods

The story of Adam and Eve, of paradise on earth, of an age in which human beings were androgynous and lived in harmony with nature and with themselves, has accompanied and stimulated for thousands of years the intuition of believers in religion, esotericists and philosophers for millennia.

All scholars of ancient toponymy agree that the term "Eden" can be traced back to the ancient Greek "Eden", whose meaning is a garden of delights.

In all the stories, both in the East and in the West, there are traces of ancient teachings that repeat recollections of a lost land, of original humanity that vibrated in unison with the cosmos. Memories of a great, evolved civilisation, destroyed by great cataclysms, are once again incredibly topical.

Scholars such as Robert Bauval have shown that the dating of events as conceived by modern scholars is totally unfounded and the monuments at Giza should be backdated at least 10,000 years.

The existence of such a civilisation is already sufficiently proven, even if fragments of deviant masonry, accomplices of the powers of the various religions, do all they can to conceal the evidence. Our intention is not to put forward that which has been developed using logical and coherent paths by respected scholars of the subject.

Rather, it is a matter of understanding the real dimension in which the inhabitants of Atlantis lived. We will once more use the knowledge handed down by the ancients, scientific findings, logic and intuition in order to produce a succinct effort that does not aim to exhaust all the questions that remain open, but above all focusses on the essential issues that we intend to discuss.

The first consideration must be on the condition of planet Earth a very long time ago.

Ancient teachings tell us that the different nature of electromagnetic forces made physical bodies lighter. Human beings were androgynous, they didn't need to reproduce, the activity of the chakras moved on the basis of the same centripetal force that moves the cosmos, the bodies were substantiated by a fine aether, which nowadays is invisible to us, nature expressed its creative force in a luminous dimension and its four elements worked together from one magnificence to another.

More than walking, human beings vibrated in the air. The legend of the dragonfly man draws its origin from this ancient knowledge.

Then a first fall occurred.

A group of entities decided to exploit the powers of the ego and enter into an autonomous path of knowledge.

During this phase, the physical body became denser, the separation between the sexes occurred, as well as the separation between the two hemispheres of the brain, movement started to become heavier and mankind touched the material surface of the Earth in order to move.

However, human beings were still light enough to move in leaps. The vital centre and the power of knowledge were still delegated to few.

During this phase, Science, Art and Religion were born, although they were not instruments divided by a dialectic of the opposites, but rather were united in a single great teaching capable of treating the vital centres of the mind and heart as one.

The two sanctuaries found their balance in the pituitary gland. The front and rear lobes of the pituitary interacted perfectly with the pineal gland.

The creative and processing parts interacted in a synthesis that allowed emotions to support the process of understanding phenomena.

We are told that this first phase is the golden age or garden of the Gods.

However, a second fall occurred. Mankind abused its powers and caused explosions that drove him into a lower vibrational dimension. Hence, the primitive man of modern science was born, lucifer, the bearer of light fallen into the dialectic of conflicts and duality, forced to undergo a painful experience in the animal world.

This chronology of events is, in some way, reflected in the scientific intuitions that escape the decadent and indoctrinated classrooms of official academies.

If we overlook the aethereal dimension of a presumed original humanity that lived in a universe parallel to ours, a theory that cannot be proven with the tools of knowledge currently available to us, the same cannot be said for the subsequent golden age, traces of which can be clearly found in the most recent discoveries.

The myth of "a golden lineage of mortal men" from whom the Gods who lived on Olympus descended, and of a time when peace and freedom from fatigue reigned, until the theft of fire by Prometheus, which marked the final fall, can be found in the legendary works of the poets and writers of antiquity, including Hesiod and Virgil.

The experience of modern man, linked more to the use of the left side of the brain, does not allow us to understand that the authors of these ancient stories were actually inspired by a creative intuition that is no less true than mathematical equations!

In any case, nowadays paleoanthropology, a science that studies the origins of the human species through the cross-reference of data from various scientific branches, helps us to gain a better understanding by comparing ancient knowledge and modern science.

It came to the following conclusions: the term "paradise" derives from the Greek "paradeisos" and from the Hebrew "pardes", and its exact meaning is "fruit tree garden", i.e. orchard. In that era, mankind only consumed fruit.

This fortunate age developed into an orchard-based ecosystem, in the modern-day Rift Valley, which the Bible calls the Valley of Eden, where modern science discovered the first traces of the human species.

Mankind moved away from its lands of origin due to the first ice age and was forced to consume other fruits, too.

The Bible is extremely clear on this point:

Every plant yielding seed that is on the surface of all the earth, and every tree which has fruit yielding seed; it shall be food for you.

The idea of a fortunate age, free of disease, of wars, of slavery from work, where mind and heart proceeded in unison, is no longer merely the preserve of ancient legends or philosophical extravagances, but a realisation accepted by a section of the modern scientific world, partially based on molecular biophysics, which is part of an overall vision and free of prejudices.

After all, if there is a truth, it can only be one and, consequently, the conclusions can only end up being identical whatever the means employed to search for it.

The dominant race

Legends tell us that after the second fall of the Gods, and the cataclysms that followed, some groups of humans dispersed in various areas of the planet.

According to some studies on the human gene, there is mapping that follows the same route in several populations located in various corners of the planet. This genetic cross-breeding can be found in the inhabitants of Peru and Mexico, in some groups in Indochina, in the Tibetan populations and in some strains of the inhabitants of the Congo.

One clear aspect is that these populations also have physical structures with similar basic traits.

However, it cannot be held that human being with these features have dominated the last 6000 years of history!

Evidently, something else occurred that modified the original genetic structure allowing the new Jewish race to take political and financial control of the planet.

Who, though, makes up the Jewish race?

The Jews are not a population that has been relegated to a corner of Palestine and that goes under the name of Israel. Many confuse Zionism with Judaism.

All Western and most Eastern populations are descendants of the Jewish race.

Judaism is not a culture, nor a people, but a race! This statement is, of course, free of any ties to the sad and nefarious outcome of Nazism. It is simply a question of identifying the passage between the descendants of Atlantis and the new emerging race from which the vast majority of Western and non-Western populations originate.

Where does the Jewish race come from?

The ancient legend of the Nephilim comes to our aid and provides us with a plausible and exhaustive explanation. The etymological root of Nephilim is "to fall", so much so that it is said that the Nephilim were giants descended from heaven, fallen angels!

When men began to multiply on the face of the land and daughters were born to them, the sons of God saw that the daughters of men were fair, and they took wives of all they desired and chose... There were giants in the earth in those days...   (Genesis)

Who were the sons of God?

Without wishing to undertake an interpretive study of the sacred texts, which nowadays are no longer relevant, could it be possible to believe that those sons of God, and therefore the Nephilim, were entities from more evolved planes of existence? Could this genetic cross-breeding have been the origin of a new human race?

We will never have proof, but logical reasoning would lead us to think that something happened, a genetic accident that produced a new race that has governed the planet for the last 6,000 years.

The Reptilian, in other words... the pelvis and the heart

In UFO mythology, a Reptilian is a being from Alpha Draconis, a constellation of the Dragon.

They are described as entities lacking in compassion and respect for other living beings, devoted to passion rather than sentimentality, driven by vital impulses towards greed, aspiration to domination and possession, full of greed and inclined to unbridled hedonism.

It is not necessary to explore Alpha Draconis or the potential characteristics of its inhabitants that may have cross-bred with the beings on the planet Earth! Indeed, our planet is full of Reptilians and they are most probably the imaginative projection of our fragment of humanity, of the true dominant race of the last millennia!

Unlike mammals, reptiles are characterised by quick reflexes, speed of execution and ruthlessness in making their vital impulse or their own elementary desires prevail.

These personalities have a poor relationship with sleep and sometimes, perhaps often, use stimulant drugs or alcohol, cultivate ambition, are in continuous competition with others, but are also susceptible and cynical.

They do not like to use too much reasoning, but rely on instinct, they ignore moral censures to reach their goals and are obsessed with money, sex and food. They sometimes or often verge on megalomania, surround themselves with vassals as kings do, or are actually kings, they search for possessions and power, they are extrovert, communicative, leaders and magnetic, but they also know how to cry and maintain an outward façade!

They are moved by ancestral forces that originate from the pelvis that drive and support them in an existence conceived as a battlefield.

However, they use heart chakras to the advantage of their plans with the power of passion and are lovers who are as involving as they are ruthless.

Obviously, as in all similar planes of reality, there are different evolutionary levels.

Therefore, they span from cruel dictators who does not hesitate to use violence and death against their opponents, successful entrepreneurs capable of overcoming any moral censure in order to achieve their goals, cynical politicians, rampant professionals, artists able to capture crowds, almost as though inspired by dark powers, and religious fanatics.

Indeed, all these figures have a single common denominator: a thirst for power and the absolute affirmation of their ego.

Reptilians do not love solitude, they need to be in contact with groups of people on whom they can exercise leadership or domination, and through which they can reflect their own narcissism.

The great minds that perform the urban planning of modern cities, conceived as hives, or design, so that they may then be built, the tallest towers are Reptilian! There are cities entirely designed on this concept and the new part of Dubai is a striking example.

What could appear as a symbol of progress and evolution is actually a plastic testament to undoubted involution!

The construction of modern cities and the ecological disasters that tend to wipe out the traces of our history are proportional to an increasingly unbridled arms race and increasingly efficient weapons of mass destruction.

A type of humanity that still coexists with wars and the atomic bomb is undoubtedly not an evolved humanity!

However, returning to the characteristics of these personalities, it must be said that once they identify with a certain environment, they suffer from traumatic detachment if they are forced to leave it.

There is nothing more painful for Reptilians than having to abandon their group and be forced into live in an environment in which nobody recognises them.

That is why, despite loving travel for pleasure, this race does not like to go far from its places of origin. If they go through a dark period, it is difficult to see them surrender, preferring to continue fighting to their last breath, even if it drives them to insanity.

It was this type of human that produced the legends of warriors, conquerors and heroes. Heroism is a mask through which the ego can elevate vanity and pride.

Conversely, boredom, dissatisfaction and frustration are the other side of the coin.

In fact, Reptilians are unable to organise their existence and achieve their successes, or simply fulfil their desires, without the help of thinking beings who plan life with rigour and precision, dispassion and detachment and elevate the qualities of reasoning.

Just as entrepreneurs cannot do without good managers, Reptilians cannot do without Greys. That's why Reptilians and Greys must necessarily walk hand in hand.

The Greys...the mind and the pelvis

Ufologists, or scholars of extra-terrestrial races, describe Greys as beings from the Zeta Reticuli system.

In UFO mythology, Reptilians created the Grey aliens as a race of slaves who, thanks to their technology, rebelled against their creators in order to travel the cosmos in search of a new home.

They have telepathic abilities, but do not possess an emotional side. They therefore appear unmoved by moods, whether their own or those of humans. They appear to act according to a collective mentality and in the interests of their group.

Their aims are pursued at a totally practical level, devoid of any sentimental involvement. Their lips are thin, their appearance stiff, their eyes cold and expressionless.

A defect in the structure of their aetheric bodies makes humanity desirable and that would seem to justify numerous human abductions aimed at creating hybrids capable of ensuring the survival of their species.

Greys are sad beings, they never smile, live in a state of worry and anguish, planning their lives solely for practical purposes.

Our world is full of beings belonging to this race.

The world of high finance and banking is governed by them, as is the organisation of the bureaucratic machinery and part of politics.

In general, they are introverted beings, dressed in sombre fashion, they rarely laugh, are often shy, are not great communicators, but are good at planning.

Their kindness is superficial, their coldness disarming and their computational ability impressive.

Although lacking in charisma, they exercise power in an occult manner, manage Masonic meetings and are rigorous in their respect of all protocols required by civil coexistence, from religiously going to mass, without being involved in it, to taking part in all official ceremonies.

They speak in a calm, slow, scientific and cynical manner.

Greys occupy the main positions of power serving the great financial powers (Reptilians) and they govern the country's major institutions.

Their eyes betray a life without light, an arid existence in which imagination loses all meaning.

The city of Geneva is symbolic of a grey aura that runs through the hearts of its citizens.

Cohabitating with a Grey person means running the risk of losing the joy of life.

For Greys, pleasure lies in possessing hidden power, in the organised manipulation of the collective subconscious, in planning strategies for controlling the masses, in perfecting models in which to identify themselves.

Their problem is certainly not that of awakening consciences, but rather that of putting them to sleep and governing them.

This millennium has seen humanity's level of collective consciousness fall to an unprecedented state of uniformity.

Greys are the planners of the dogmas with which entire masses of fanatical men are kept imprisoned, as well the governors of those scientific congresses which promote distorted truths in bad faith.

The Greys are turning people into machines through the systematic manipulation of dynamics with which the system transforms human beings into little more than robots, through a continuous rhythm of repetitive behaviour that we persist in calling life.

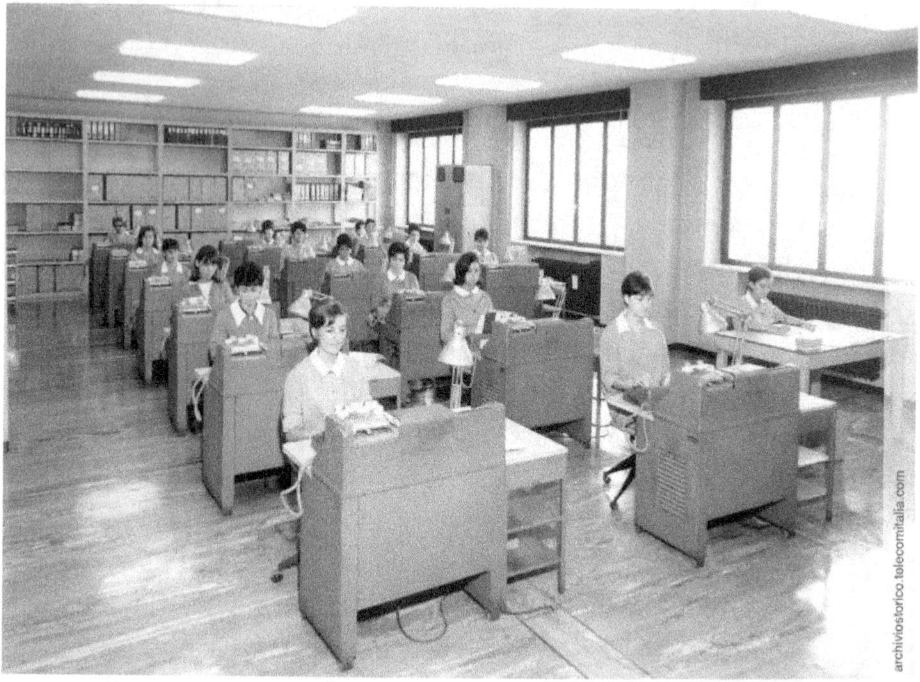
archiviostorico.telecomitalia.com

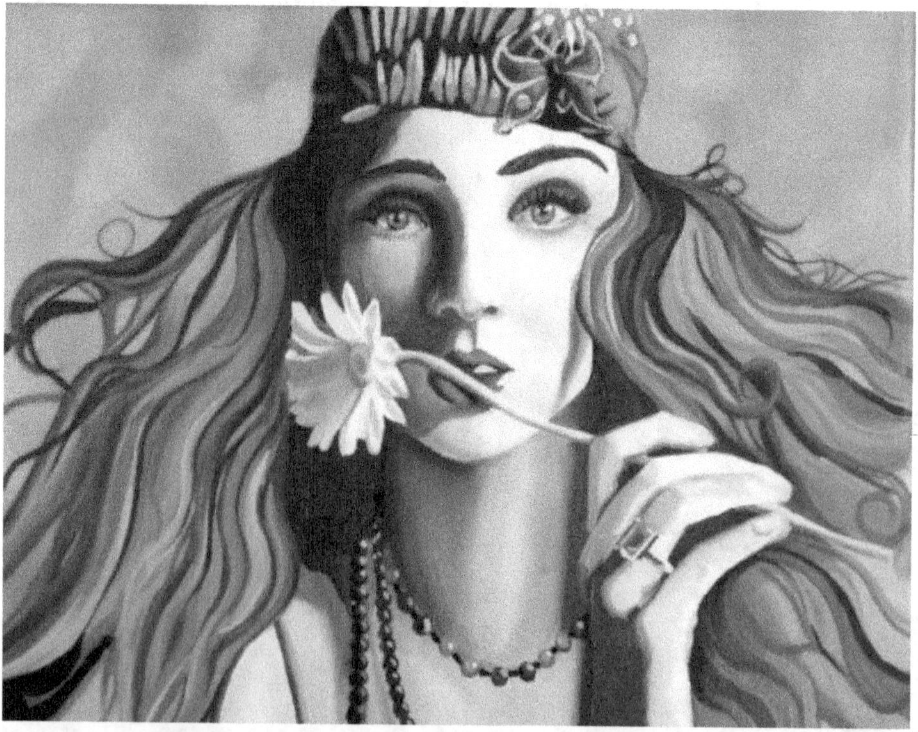

The Nordics, the heart and the mind

In UFO mythology, Nordics are a race which hails from the Pleiades, in the Taurus constellation.

They are believed to be very similar to humans and resemble certain Nordic populations, among which they could easily disguise their presence.

It is no coincidence that we believe this race to be the closest, even in physical terms, to the human race. Nordics are exactly how we would like to be.

Tall, blond, fair complexion, great intelligence and sensitivity, great love for the universe and life, high level of spirituality, sense of peace, altruism and a sense of art and music.

Exactly how we would like to be!

By that, I'm not excluding their existence a priori, but there is no doubt that Nordics represent the unquestionable projection of our frustrated desires.

After all, many human beings tend to lie in a state of being that is closer to a quality of life and a cultural vision of things aimed at freeing the animal instinct so that it may aspire to greater awareness, as well as transcending the forces of the pelvis in the chakras of the heart and mind.

Among them, in a less evolved dimension, we find artists who try to reproduce the vibrations of the universe using sound, intellectuals who are curious about parallel worlds, philanthropists who are always attentive to the needs of people, idealists who believe they are fighting for a just cause, dreamers who feel alien to a perverse social organisation.

We can attribute the hippy movement in the Sixties and the subsequent New Age to these types of person who interact, or believe they do, with invisible worlds from which they draw inspiration.

They govern the controversial planet of teachers, gurus and yogis.

There are true seekers among them, driven by a sincere need to discover the essence of things, but who very often remain trapped in the walls of Ephesus, the city at the border.

Transcendental meditation, so widespread in the West, is a typical example of how personalities aspire to rise above an ordinary dimension imbued with conflicts and contradictions.

However, the ego is contradiction and conflict and, therefore, very often, except in very rare cases, such attempts are destined to come up against the illusion of progressing to more advanced worlds.

Nordics, in their most evolved state, are like John the Baptist, who, at some point in his life, found that he was in a desert. Only in that precise moment, after long, difficult and tormented wanderings, is the personality ready to meet Arcas.

The Arcturians... the perfect union

Some scholars of ufology believe that the Arcturians are among the most advanced extra-terrestrial races known, capable of living simultaneously in multi-functional universes.

Arcturians apparently have magical powers, and their extremely high level of spirituality places them among the inhabitants of a parallel universe 'whose gateway is the blue planet orbiting the red star Arcturus in the Boötes constellation.

Our planet has also known many sons of Arcas. There is no doubt that all the great messengers who introduced universal teachings, which were subsequently betrayed by natural religions, drew their wisdom from dimensions of consciousness unrelated to the ego and this dimensional plane.

Arthur's kingdom is not of this world and only those willing to sacrifice their ego on the altar of truth can hope to enter it.

Arcturians act in an impersonal manner and never behave like a teacher or a spiritual point of reference.

They are aware of the science of intercosmic radiation and their personality, purified by conditioning, becomes a receptive antenna to keep field of energy alive as the only true instrument of genuine seekers.

Hence, many have been summoned by this electromagnetic field from a parallel universe, but few are the chosen ones.

The teachings of Arcturians stand out because they never tend to inflate the ego or recommend evolutionary paths.

The path taken by Arcturians is a journey to destroy the conditioning power of a blocked vibratory dimension that brings death and pain.

Arcturians know that this world, even on its most evolved planes, even in its most resplendent ages, is bound by the power of death.

True students of Arcturian teachings, although peaceful beings who are devoid of aggression, have often been persecuted in mankind's history and often crucified.

The great massacres carried out by the Catholic Church against unarmed populations, guilty merely of professing and confessing original Christian teachings, are just one of the examples of a dramatic story in which the persecuted and the persecutors, inventors of dogmas capable of imprisoning consciences and seekers of the truth can be found in every era.

The legend of King Arthur and the twelve knights of the round table symbolically represents the magical epic of Arcas' message.

The twelve knights represent the twelve cranial nerves that serve King Arthur, the awakened consciousness, and the battlefield is no longer the external dimension of things, but the path of self-knowledge and the destruction of the conditioning power of the past, a path not without pitfalls, conflicts and pain.

Only the death of King Arthur frees the knights of the round table, through a transfiguristic epic that leading them to the lands of Avalon, after the power of the Grail has fully entered the vital circuits of a renewed personality.

Therefore, the round table is our brain. The twelve knights are the twelve cranial nerves. Arthur is the ego that governs the vital system through the hypophysis. His death is also a rebirth. The new vibrational dimensions of another universe dance in unison and the hypophysis transcends into a new field of consciousness, in which the three chakras regain lost unity, see new heavens and new lands.

The same symbolic representation of the journey towards dimensions that appear mysterious to laymen can be found in all the great teachings. The gospel, now no longer relevant, represents the same identical path.

Jesus was born in a stable in Bethlehem, the heart, the seat of a vital beginning, the only vestige of original mankind.

His path led him to Jerusalem, the head, where he taught the twelve disciples, the twelve cranial nerves, and led them to a higher dimension of consciousness through the crucifixion of the hypophysis. This is where the union of the front and rear lobes stimulate the pineal, whose awakening activates the electromagnetic circuits that elevate the entire vital system to a different and rediscovered sensory capacity.

The twelve signs of the zodiac also symbolically represent the path of the ego, from the *I am* of Aries to the *I die unto myself* of Pisces. There are twelve months in a year and there are twelve hours on a clock face: coincidence?

Unfortunately, these teachings have been disfigured, corrupted and mystified throughout the last centuries by the powerful, who have grasped the task of reigning over fallen humanity.

The dominant mystique and conditioning of reassuring natural churches, humanity's tendency to seek external guides and convenient paradises have made the most ardent of seekers and the most genuine of teachings yield to the temptation of hierarchical organisations that only end up representing a limit for a journey trapped in the perverse laws of time.

Arcturians do not give up!

In one way or another, they keep the bridge that connects our lives to our home of origin open.

In so doing, Arcturians exercise compassion, a spirit of service that paints existence in extraordinary and shimmering colours.

The open well

In the lines of argument, as dealt with so far, we have sought a point of contact between the great philosophical and mysterious teachings.

However, there is an attempt in the background at a vision of things that is free of the stereotypes and images engrained in our genetic mapping and the millennial power of conditioning.

We have left the field open to observing the great mysteries that envelop humanity and combining them with our cognitive power.

We have discovered that the possible existence of aetheric worlds is the basis of great religious mystifications and that which belongs to the invisible world is no less real than that which involves dense matter.

We have revisited the stages of the evolution of mankind, knowing that the three vital centres that characterise the personality are disunited, resulting in wars, destruction and pain.

We have mentioned an alternative vision of the human races and discovered those that dominate the world scene nowadays.

Lastly, we have hypothesised that messengers from a parallel universe leave the field open to a vibrational circuit and electromagnetic currents capable of shaking the most sensitive personalities and leaving the door of a different dimension of existence open.

I think it's worth exploring this point in order to gain a better understanding of what is currently happening on our planet.

Let's imagine opening a well that has been closed and covered for years and doing so in daytime, say on a beautiful sunny day.

The light filtering through produces a sort of insane activity among the thousands of insects and larvae that lived in darkness.

If these predators of the water surface had an autonomous consciousness, they might think that a divine light entered their vital system.

The light produces two separate consequences. For some, there is death and destruction, while for others, who endure it, there is the rebirth of a new life made of light and no longer of darkness.

Any reasonable observer of the event would know all of the above.

Sunlight is simply the sun's light, but for the poor larva it is a disconcerting or a salvific event, one that is incomprehensible, because it is invisible to its state of consciousness. It senses its effects, but cannot understand its cause.

Hence, if a light from an electromagnetic force that is different to the one we know penetrates our planetary system, we would not be able to see it, because we lack the sensory tools to do so, but we would feel its effects, just like the tadpoles in the well that has been opened.

Many postulate a cosmic scenario that, according to the laws of the time, involves certain appointments after several millennia.

Now, just as the light of the sun shines more at its zenith in the microcosm of Earth, we cannot rule out that the same thing is accomplished in a cosmic cycle and that said appointment ends up determining a flow of electromagnetic rays of greater intensity, such as to flood the entire solar system with intense energy.

In esoteric teachings, reference is often made to the succession of the various astrological eras and to the various energy fields that also influence terrestrial mankind.

Our civilisation was born on the banks of Egypt around 6000 years ago. In fact, recent geological and archaeological studies are unveiling the probable existence of older civilisations, up to about 12,000 years ago.

A study by Robert Bauval on the Sphinx is extraordinarily significant in this sense and has revolutionised the grey maps on which our more recent history was too hastily, or deliberately, written.

Therefore, with the advent of the Age of Aquarius, the planet is apparently crossing a cosmic space in which light is more intense, to the extent that it is opening the well that kept us in the shade.

In modern science, answers to causes are identified through the sort of logical reasoning that identifies answers in the effects.

The turning point of our solar system, as well as of planet Earth, reproduces something that has already happened before and that will happen again. The inhabitants of the solar system are exposed more intensely to inter-cosmic rays from an unknown source.

In fact, the rays are provoking a general disorientation in humanity, increasing the number of conflicts and wars, selfishness goes beyond the limits of natural tolerance, the collective ego seems to travel towards nothingness, a helpless witness to the demolition of all the masks it had worn over the centuries.

It replicates exactly what happened to the tadpoles exposed to the sun's rays once the well was opened.

The source can only originate from the vibrational fields of another cosmic dimension, in that bridge that remains open thanks to the sense of compassion of free entities that exist outside our laws.

That is why all ancient texts often refer to the illusion of time, to the concept of eternity and to an awakening.

This light, this invisible energy, these rays are here either for the purposes of resurrection or a final fall!

That is why it is said that:

My kingdom is not of this world... I have not come to bring peace... whoever loses their life for My sake will save it.

In the midst of all this confluence of cosmic laws is a perfect balance that obviously does not take into account our thinking, but flows with absolute perfection in the manifestation of creation.

Therefore, according to this vision, God does not exist, being a primitive and decadent projection of false teachers.

Instead, there is Love, which has nothing to do with the sentimentality and the passion with which most of mankind plays, but is understood as being a great source of light that has been and will be, and which brings the living entity that is enveloped by it back to the tabernacle of the Gods.

Indeed, when we feel irrepressible nostalgia for something we do not know, it is Life that is seeking its flow and the garden of the Gods is its destiny.

The atom, the various fields of consciousness

The subject matter that forms the basis of creation has been discussed for millennia. Leaving aside the various theories, from Democritus to Epicurus, on which the various hypotheses were founded regarding the elements that constituted our essence, it is clear that interpretive unilateralism has given way to concepts shared by the entire scientific community. The physicist Rutherford, in the early nineteenth century, put forward the model of an atom that had a nucleus as its centre and electrons as the particles that revolved around it, just like a sun orbited by planets. This theory, which was confirmed by several experiments, was only partially revisited subsequently, but never refuted.

Hence, if 'on earth as it is in heaven' is true, we can assume that an atom possesses all the elements on which our existence as we know it is founded.

The atom is a microcosm with a central element, the nucleus, around which various particles attracted and supported by its light rotate.

In scholastic teaching, it has always been claimed that there are three elements that make up the atom: the nucleus, the electrons and the protons.

That which had initially seemed indivisible, then appeared divisible, to the extent that the schizophrenia of brutal modern science is oriented towards experiments aimed at isolating the various sub-particles that make up the central elements, in search of the particle of God!

Another interesting aspect is the presence of a dark space, defined as an empty space, in the atom, exactly as it appears in the visible configuration of our matter.

Thanks to so-called quantum theory, science began to penetrate the unexplored space of vibrational frequencies.

Research first performed by Max Planck and, subsequently, by Einstein, placed the emphasis is on the corpuscular nature of light, and the hypothesis was that the kinetic energy of the electrons did not depend, as claimed by traditional theories, on the intensity of the radiation emitted by a source of light – the photoelectric effect -, but rather on its frequency. This can only be understood if the atom's black body, i.e. its empty space, is taken into consideration.

Indeed, experiments showed that the intensity of the radiation emitted went beyond the normally known peaks, up to increasingly higher frequencies that can no longer be monitored.

Without wishing to enter into academic areas that are not part of the author's field of knowledge, two pieces of data emerge from these increasingly perfected studies: "matter is energy" and "there is no empty space"!

Not only that, but the ancient concepts of traditional physics on time and space are questioned and enucleated in a new realisation that suggests our field of observation is "relative", in the sense that our observation of physical phenomena, considered the sensory tools that are available to us, is incomplete and partial.

Hence, this kind of simplification, which could give the keepers of scientific power and official knowledge quite a start, clearly explains the manipulation to which the masses are subjected.

Indeed, extremely simple concepts, which can be found in texts as early as those of the ancient Sumerians, are the subject of sophisticated scientific investigations and debates which take only take part in certain congresses. However, if you ask a high school student to explain them, they will encounter all sorts of difficulties.

The method remains unvaried: the use of terminological formalism and, when necessary, the interpretations of paid charlatans on TV to distort concepts that, when discussed from a holistic cultural perspective, would undermine all knowledge on which the entire system of school programmes is based, in which minds are shaped according to an increasingly conformed and one-sided vision.

Yet studies on the atom, when removed from a purely scientific perspective and seen on the ampler level of the interpretation of reality, confirm the ancient teachings of Hermes Trismegistus: 'on earth as it is in heaven', on the inside as it is on the outside, nothing is created and nothing is destroyed!

Our spaces are therefore equipped with various frequency fields, the space that appears empty to us is, on the contrary, animated by various sources of life and energy, the dark and black space of the atom is merely that which we call the beyond, understood as beyond that which we see and know.

The various vibrations give rise to various energy fields that are the source of many states of evolution and consciousness.

There are no inter-dimensional spaces within our universe, but only forms of life vibrating on quantum energy with scales of frequencies.

For example, using another frequency would allow beings from other areas of known space to widen or narrow the space-time boundaries and reach our planet via spiral waves. Exactly as happens in the microcosm of an atom!

The universe in which we live is based on a single law, it is a large atom with various life forms on various levels of vibrational scales that are more or less advanced and of which we inhabitants of the Earth have only an extremely limited vision, given that mankind is not endowed with sensory tools capable of interacting with all the various planes of existence.

However, the atom is divisible and therefore devoid of that longed-for unity in which opposites, and therefore the conflict between the various elements, extend towards the territories of peace.

Hence, our universe is limited, it is the city of Ephesus.

Therefore, there must be something else that goes beyond the visible and invisible spaces of our cosmic dimension and, if that were the case, that something must necessarily be composed of matter consisting of various particles, which are alien to the atom as we know it.

That is why the search for the particle of God inside the atomic structure of this matter is merely the perverse game of devious minds.

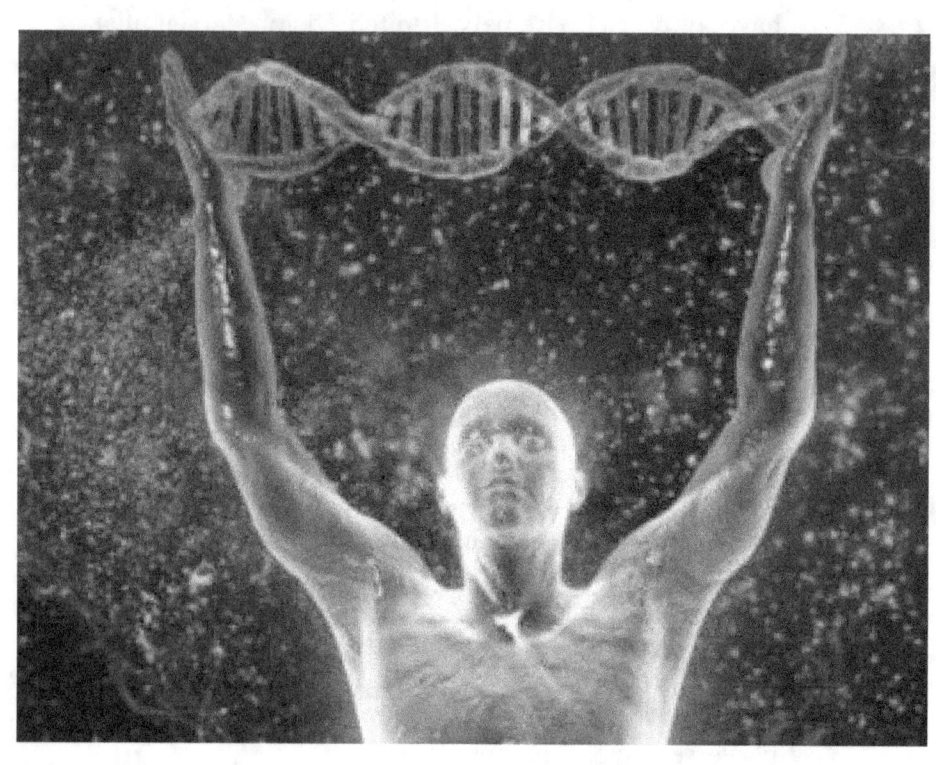

The cornerstone: the coincidence of all teachings

In the beginning was the Word, and the Word was with God, and the Word was God... In him was life, and that life was the light of all mankind. (The gospel of Jhon)

Therefore, in the beginning there was the original atom, which constituted the essence of the realm of origins and already contained all the principles of creation, within it were life and unity, and that life was the light of original mankind.

If there is therefore a parallel universe, the seat of a unitary life, made of light and creativity and in which opposites come together, it must be made of a different substance and according to a principle that, unlike this type of atom, is supported by a centripetal force.

It is the original atom, the divine principle, the end of good and evil, Eden.

All the ancient teachings, subsequently mystified by religions and their symbols, coincide remarkably on this point.

There is a "divine principle" inside us, an original atom that caused the spark, as a bridge to the parallel universe.

All the mystery schools and the science of true alchemy are based on this knowledge.

A journey leading to the awakening of this energy source must make it possible to renew the atomic structure of our being and find ourselves spontaneously in a dimension of consciousness in which the chakras unite and matter vibrates with another substance.

This original principle evidently is not related to the various animist currents found in the various religions.

Therefore, as admirably described in Cristiano Rosacroce's alchemical wedding, the only Temple is our body.

Awakening coincides with the realisation of a limited perception of phenomena, and our existence, unmasked of all illusions, becomes a desert to be crossed in order to reach the Promised Land.

Our mind is far from the truth simply because it is confused by too much information, much of which was subsequently transformed into images.

That is why the ancient teachings may no longer provide the key to opening the portal of the mystery. The Gautama Buddha reminded us that «better than possessing the whole world, better than paradise, better than dominion over all the worlds... is taking the first step on the road to awakening».

However, that awakening is a word that has been manipulated by too many interpreters throughout history and is no longer relevant, just like the Holy Scriptures.

Reflect, therefore, and be sure one day not to regret having allowed this doctrine to spread in an unworthy manner. The best way to keep them will be not to write them down, but to learn them and put them into practice ourselves!

Plato had hit the mark, so much so that his concept of platonic love, understood as an intermediary between this universe and the original one, i.e. like the force field between the various dimensions, has become a joke of trivial sentimentality!

This symbolism was a way of expressing extraordinary truths in a historical moment of human evolution in which certain messages could only be understood through the chakra of the heart.

Those maps are now old and yellowed, influenced by millennia of misleading interpretations.

Leaving historical eras aside, according to elementary logic, this path must have been and will only be possible thanks to electromagnetic radiation originating from another universe, capable of such an awakening, in as much as they are similar to the original atomic principle.

The cornerstone is within us, it is an atom of a different nature, the holy Grail, on which the true builders can work using the only tool available to us, the photonic light source that compassionately courses through our lives, indifferent to human vanity, far from good and evil, as conceived by us. At the cinema, the images projected are separate from the viewer, but if we watch a 3D film, we find ourselves at the centre of the scene through the use of a sensory tool.

This applies exactly to the various fields of perception. We perceive everything around us as something separate from us.

A different level of perception would provide us with another representation of reality, in which we would feel part of every phenomenon, and any sense of separation would cease. This state of "ecstasy" is not a consequence of an exhilarating mystical path, but of the reopening of a cerebral portal. This can only happen through the rays of love nurtured in the infinity.

Therefore, if it is true that in this particular cosmic time the planet is experiencing a more intense source of light, it is also true that the chances of spontaneously fostering the great possibility that lies within us increase. On ancient maps, this possibility is described as a hard journey of sacrifice, like an ordeal. They are suggestions based on millennia of iconoclastic conditioning. Nothing could be further from the truth!

"We all have a duty to learn again the lost and forgotten liberating Word. When the Sacred Language of all times speaks of the unique Word of God, it does not mean a collection of writings of greater or lesser value whose meaning has been degraded or distorted, but the Word of Life, unique and liberating, the path, the method, the holy science that leads to the Universal Life of the immutable Kingdom. "

(Jan van Riickenborgh, Catharose de Petri)

Prisoners of a spell: neuronal deconditioning

It is possible to see the digital fingerprint of the past in every personality. That past is its conditioning. We are children of our genetic mapping, of the environment in which we live, of the culture we acquire.

Conditioning has millennial internal roots, but also external roots that depend on ethnic, racial and geographical factors. To gain a better understanding of the roots of conditioning, we need to explore the laws of causality.

The principle of physics by which every action has an equal and opposite reaction comes from incontrovertible empirical data.

If I throw a stone into a pond, the strength of water's movement will be proportional to the qualitative and quantitative impulse of the contraction medium.

This principle gives rise to the other predominant theory for which no effect can occur before a cause, but must necessarily be a consequence.

The principle of causality establishes that it is not possible to consider cause and effect in an inverted temporal order, in any reference system, since the simultaneous dynamics of events cannot be altered.

Therefore, it is not possible to transcend these concepts, provided they are closely linked to those of time and space as we know them. Hence, when we talk about conditioning, we refer to an impulse that comes from the past and produces a certain effect in the immediate present.

Paradoxically, the present is therefore the direct consequence of our past. Sciences such as astrology are based on this law. The study of the stars is merely the auric reading of electromagnetic impulses from our past.

If the past is our conditioning, the present does not exist until it frees itself from the weight of the past!

This path is described in all ages as the only true path to freedom. If we free ourselves from the chains of the past, mankind no longer sees the shadows of reality, but sees reality itself!

This encounter is described in early mythologies in various ways, from the myth of Plato's cave onwards, but the common sense is the representation of a state of consciousness that overcomes the barriers of the known in order to explore the infinite universe of the eternal present.

This path of deconditioning, unlike the one that is often promoted, is merely an abdication of one's own habits and one's own thoughts.

When a personality detaches itself from its ordinary paths by sacrificing reason to the spirit of truth, something extraordinary happens.

The neuronic system is oriented in another direction, just like leaves turning towards the light. Until recently, it was believed that, once destroyed, neurons did not reproduce.

Nowadays, neurogenesis has re-assessed this concept and, on the basis of specific experiments, is ready to recognise the possibility of a renewal of the brain cells and therefore of the entire related nervous system.

Habits are interconnected with the nervous apparatus that, on the basis of impulses written in our genetic masses, tend to raise defensive barriers and resist change.

While the reaction is justified on a physical level due to a physiological need for self-protection, the question changes when it comes to psychological reactions.

The dynamics of the latter depend on the memory of what has been and therefore the challenges are always new, but the reactions remain the same!

Consider the enormous drama of war that mankind is unable to free itself from. Faced with an interpersonal conflict, we usually react with verbal or physical aggression.

Obviously, this primitive state of consciousness also applies to major political and social processes.

The atomic bomb is the extreme synthesis of our impotence. The larger and more powerful the nuclear devices, the smaller and more insignificant the components of the human race become.

If we do not have the courage to acknowledge that unfortunately our vital dimension and our level of consciousness are only slightly more evolved than those of other forms of terrestrial animals, and we continue to confuse technological progress with an intelligent view of phenomena, we end up neglecting the enormous potential that we know lies in the secrets of our body and that could allow us to lift the veil of conditioning.

Neurons receive impulses from electromagnetic circuits in which experiences are recorded.

If we accustom neurons to look for the truth in things, they will register the impulse. From that moment, the sacred demon of the path towards the truth will possess us,

Arcas will be born from the secret of the heart and a new mankind will be ready for the journey. The spell will be broken and the personality thus becomes an antenna to receive permanent cosmic impulses.

Seeing is believing!

The greater the number of seekers who take Arcas' path, the more the other terrestrial races will suffer indirect consequences. That is why it is said that He came either for a fall or for a resurrection!

The powerful vibrations produced by those on the path of deconditioning end up producing beneficial explosions on the slight and aethereal planes of the planet.

The well is opened and light enters! Organisms that had hitherto been in the dark, end up stirring perpetually, either due to a new life or due to their destruction.

That is why at this particular moment in history, disease increases, anxieties take on often catastrophic proportions, right up to extreme gestures, social life seems to tread the thin line of imminent disasters of war and the planet reacts with natural disasters.

Anyone can see it happening, in front of their very eyes.

Only pompous ignorance can deny the evidence!

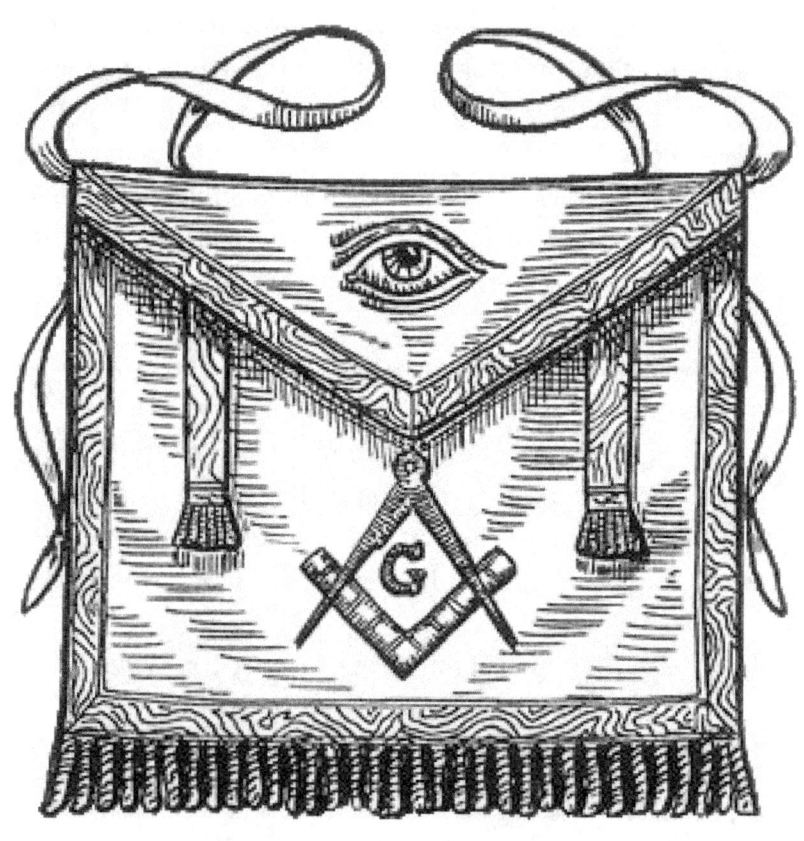

The governors of an agonising world

On 24 February 1897, on the eve of the launch of a newspaper written by free thinkers, there was a meeting in Grenoble, France, which saw all the great masters of European Freemasonry gathered together. At the time, Freemasonry wielded the occult power of political and cultural life in the more advanced countries and influenced masses of unaware citizens. Masonry was also the guardian of ancient esoteric teachings reserved for the chosen few who presumed to appreciate their essence.

An intense debate took place that day which was to change the destiny of mankind in the centuries to come.

On the one side, there were those who believed that the masses should be taught, educated and helped to evolve along a path of awareness, while on the other side, there was a majority group that believed the masses should be guided and manipulated, given that they were immune from all attempts to awaken them to a more aware dimension of existence.

In the end, after three days of intense discussions and as many breaks, a compromise was found.

Individuals from the masses would be given an opportunity to evolve and, therefore, the selection criteria of the ruling classes and so-called free spirits would become more flexible.

Masonic circles, hitherto organised on a horizontal plane, would develop vertically, through a process of aggregation that, from the bottom, would allow a more capillary control of all the apparatuses of power.

On the other hand, the systems of influence would become more incisive and determined, through the systematic use of means, including more sophisticated ones, aimed at uniforming the awareness of populations, in order to preserve and keep teaching within a restricted circle of persons capable of passing it on from generation to generation.

This assumption, devised in the pompous elitist circles and conceived as a philosophical axiom, ended up crossing the oceans of time, from century to century, until it resulted in the massification of Freemasonry at the end of the Seventies and the establishment of alternative and competing circles and movements, governed by a highly sophisticated leadership.

Its objective was to destroy the old Masonic meetings, providing the individuals from the masses who entered those cenacles with the illusion of importance, while in reality transferring the governance of the occult power elsewhere.

Nowadays, freemasonry is just a myth that has been consigned to the scholars of history or to a few deluded people who practice it for sad and modest social ambition.

Grey and Reptilian beings govern these underworlds of human existence without scruples, moved by great anguish, forced into dark and desolate nooks, in a world of darkness that no longer knows any borders.

Walking zombies succumb to these harmful influences and shapeless masses of human beings walk through life without purpose, without a defined goal. That is how the world became unmasked, now that it is devoid of art, science and culture.

That is how the grand design of a uniforming of cultural products is achieving its moment of glory at the beginning of the third millennium. It is from the effects that we discover the causes: once again, the reasoning is logical, not distorted by para-esoteric emphasis.

However, there is a power that transcends all human power and is in no way related to the dazzling primitive mysticisms to which mankind still succumbs: it is the power of slight energies.

Each one of our thoughts moves an amount of energy that is proportional to the quality of the vibrations emanated.

The more personalities take a path towards awareness and escape the aetheric prison artfully constructed over the centuries, the more the veil of lies is lifted. A group of men is enough to change the destiny of the planet or perhaps to accomplish it!

This is science, not science fiction!

Hunting for Cain

After the fall of the Gods, the first original humanity was divided into two lineages, that of Cain and that of Abel.

Abel represents individuals of the masses who venerate their own good and sacrifice their aether in one of the religions in order to serve the God of this world, Lucifer.

That which might appear a mere Gnostic influence can be found in the phenomena described above.

Individuals of the masses follow their instinct, are incessantly engaged in the preservation of their ego, enveloped in their beliefs, reassured by their material and immaterial possessions and comforted by their dogmas in an eternal conflict between a false good and a false evil, ready to worship the powerful of this world or the entities that govern the dark planes of the planet.

On the contrary, Cain are restless personalities who perceive injustice and the limit of this Nature, which is jarred by conflicts, in the continuous search for the profound Truth, solitary seekers who never find a comfortable bed in which to settle or a space in this existence in which they can finally feel at ease.

Never satiated of the sacred desire to learn, at a certain point they discover that it is not knowledge understood as the cognition of phenomena that provides the ultimate answer. Following terrible experiences and an equal amount of pain, still influenced by Abel's dictatorship, they set out on a journey in search of a place where they can find some peace, where every conflict can reach an end.

At first, the path appears complicated and the place unreachable. There is still something left to do: kill Abel's influence!

That will be the most revolutionary act, but also a great gesture of love aimed at eradicating the most hidden roots of the ego.

Hence, the birth of the cursed seeker of history, Ulysses! Along his journey, he is tempted by art and philosophy, encounters demons and witches, giants and deserted places. Often enveloped by pain, he cries out in defeat.

His cry is lost in the ocean of time, in search of his native country, his lost Ithaca, his affections subjugated to the arrogance of petulant demons.

Cain is the bearer of the sacred poison of restlessness, which is the only condition capable of unveiling the true meaning of life.

Many men are on that journey back and many have already travelled it.

However, none of them are really safe.

Today, the world is still hunting for Cain!

Thank you:

- All the seekers I met on the way.

I could have never written this book without the teachings of Lectorium Rosicrucianum and Jiddu Krishnamurti.

Pierre D'Essany is the pseudonym of the italian writer Elio D'Aquino

www.ingramcontent.com/pod-product-compliance
Lightning Source LLC
Chambersburg PA
CBHW060435290526
45791CB00002B/950